purpose to help people with any problems that may occur.

Important Sites:

http://www.pcprobsww.tk
For more troubleshooting go to this site and I will answer your problems as best I can.

.

Dedications

For Mrs Grover, for advising me to write a troubleshooting book for computers

Contents

Accessing an External Hard Drive.
More Information
What an External Hard Drive is: An external hard drive is a hard drive that is not built in to the computer (E.G: Somewhere else on the network.

My Computer

How to do it:
1. Double-click 'My Computer'
2. Double-Click the external hard drive's name.

Network Drives

 2436wilwri on '2436dc01\pupil$' (H:)

 applications$ on '2436dc01' (J:)

 Resources on '2436dc01' (R:)

 common on '2436dc01' (S:)

3. You have now accessed the External Hard Drive.

Tip: Your computer doesn't usually come with an external hard drive. So don't worry if you can't see it when you open My Computer.

Other Things to think about:
If My Computer isn't on your Desktop it will be in the Start menu!

Note: The External Hard Drive may not always be available if it is part of a bigger network or even a server!

Cell Types

What they are:

Cell types can make an Excel Cell do different things (E.G: Currency) This can be helpful if you are wanting the Pound Sign (£) to automatically appear when you start typing digits.

How to do it:

1. Right Click the cell.

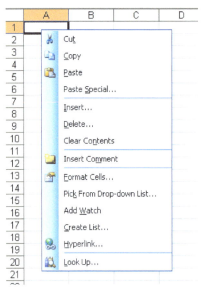

2. Click Format Cells

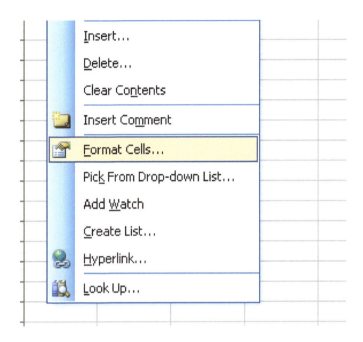

3. Now select the Cell Type and click Ok.

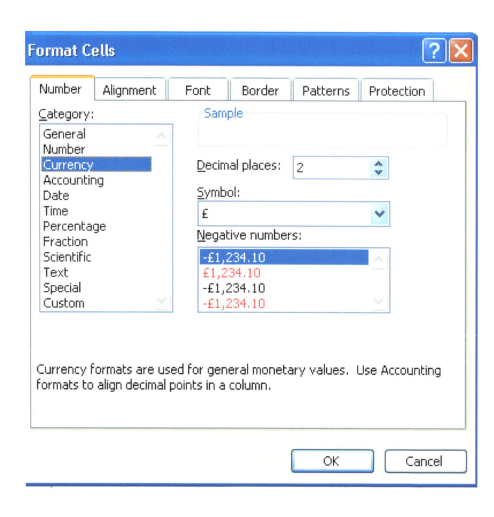

4. Now you have changed the Cell type!

Being able to see all the data in a chart.
How to do it
1. Simply click the little circle and drag outwards!
2. Now you have extended your chart and should be able to see all the information in the table/chart.

Finding Information on the Internet.
What the Internet is:
The Internet is an Information 'Gold Mine'. To find information use these method:
- Use http://www.google.co.uk

How to add headings to a table/chart

How to do it:

Enter it in the chart/table wizard!

Log-on / Turn on error

What they are:

They are errors that prevent or pause the logon sequence, meaning they ask you to do something to turn on successfully.

How to fix them:

Just select 'Start Windows normally' and push the Enter key. However if it does not say this or anything of the sort, turn off the computer and restart it. If the error continues then contact your technician or computer manufacture.

Moving Data, in cells, one or more rows or columns up or down.

What they are:

Cells are the little blocks that you see all over the Workbook, meaning the Excel screen.

How to do it:

1. Highlight all of the data in that column or row.
2. Cut the highlighted selection
3. Click the one below where the top of the data used to be and paste. You can do this for more than one cell.
4. Now you have moved the data!

<u>Opening Documents</u>
How to do it:
1. Go to the source file (The one where the file is)
2. Double-click on the file
3. The file will now open in the appropriate software.

<u>Spell Check</u>
What it is:
Spell check is a quick and easy way to check your spelling. Your computer should do it automatically, but if it does not follow this easy method.
How to Do it:
1. Click the spell check button.

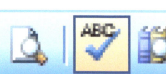

2. The incorrect spellings will be displayed in the dialog box.

3. Once you have finished checking the spellings the dialog box will disappear.

<u>**Making a picture behind text**</u>
How to do it:
1. Click the 'Little dog'.

2. Click Behind Text and then position the picture where you want it.

Entering a URL Correctly
What a URL is:

A URL is an address that you type into the internet to find a webpage. The most common URL prefix is, ' www.' And the most common suffix is ' .com'

How to Do it:

1. Open Internet Explorer (or your equivalent browser.)
2. Type the address into the address bar

3. Type the address and hit Enter.
4. The webpage will be displayed shortly.

Setting Up SWEEX Headphones

How to do it:

1. Insert the headphones into the front panel of the computer, with the pink and green sockets on (Starting with the headphones, don't put the Mic. in yet!).
2. Make sure the dialog has a tick next to the Headphones selection.

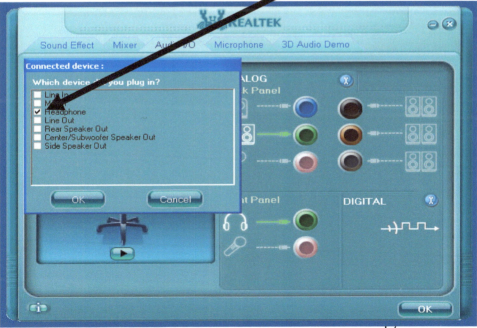

4. Repeat for the Mic.
5. You have now setup the headphones.
6. Click OK in the main setup window.

Microsoft Word

Microsoft Word is a program for writing letters, studying, writing up homework and writing books. (As I am doing now!) It is very easy to use and comes with the Microsoft Office package. Here are some common problems and how to solve them:

<u>Adding a page</u>

How to do it:

1. Press enter until a new page appears
2. You have now added a new page!

<u>Changing the font</u>

In MS Word there are hundreds of different fonts, like these:

- Helvetic
- **Impact**
- Courier
- Berlin Sans FB

How to do it:

1. Click on the font drop-down box, at the top of the page.

2. Select the font wanted.
3. Start typing in that font on the document

Changing the font already in the document

How to do it

1. Highlight the text wanted to change into the new font
2. Then change the font in the font menu (See above!)

Top Tip for Word

Always save your work as you go along, because if MS Word crashes you may lose your work!

Computer top tips.

Here are some top tips for operating a computer.

1. Always save your work; if your computer crashes and you have not saved your work you may lose everything!

2. Treat computers with respect; they cost a lot of money so make sure you use the properly or they may break.

3. If you are on a school, or business server, then make sure you use that for what you have been set to do; or you may get into trouble with your network administrator.

4. If you own a laptop, then remember to always turn it off when you have done with it. As it may get very hot and overheat, causing data loss, and maybe even breaking the computer.

5. If your computer does crash then don't panic, so long as you have saved your work! All you have to do is press CTRL+ALT+DELETE and that should resolve the problem. If not then do CTRL+ALT+DELETE again but click on Task Manager. Then end the Non Responding program that way.

Maintaining other Hardware

- With data projectors, they need their air filters cleaning out every month or so. Remember to do this or it may crash.
- Always remember to read the instruction manual for further instructions.

Creating a free website

Many people now have their own website. Here is a guide to getting yourself a free and easy-to-use one.

Starting Up

Starting a webpage is the tricky bit, but following this guide you will find it so easy you could do it with your eyes closed, hopefully!

1. Go to www.yola.com
2. Click on Login, then Sign Up.

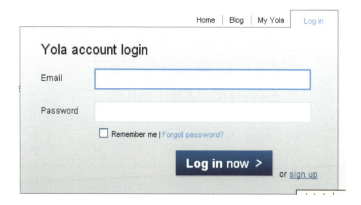

3. Follow the 'Register' wizard, you should now be taken to a page asking you to set up your site.
4. Follow the wizard and set up your site!

Editing your site

There are many of different ways editing websites, but here is the easiest way!

1. Log in to Yola, with your Username and Password.
2. Click on the blue open button
3. You can now start editing your site.

Top Tip: Always remember to republish your site every time you change something.

Top Tip: Drag-and-Drop new things on to your site to make a new impression!

Changing the domain to a shorter personal one.

Most people think that a personal domain is a pricy situation, but here is a way that is free!

1. Go to www.dot.tk
2. Type your long Yola address into the homepage
3. Then rename it and click on the Register without email button.

4. You have now renamed the domain!

PhotoStory 3

What is it :

PhotoStory 3 is a program for making stories from photos and narration, which is recorded from a microphone connected to the computer.

How to start a new project

1. Open PhotoStory 3

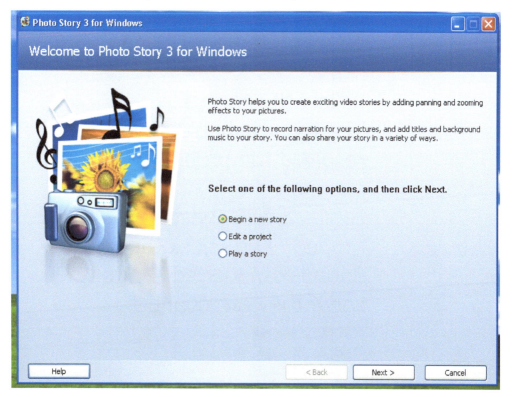

2. Select Begin New Story and follow the on-screen instructions to make your new project

Getting the narration working

1. Click the little microphone button, on the narration page, on the right hand side.
2. Follow the wizard.
3. The wizard should have resolved the problem. If not then check all the cables are connected properly and check the Sound Manager screen to see if they are connected.

(See page 8 for further information on how to complete this task.)

Completing the PhotoStory

1. Finish the wizard and save your project to a memorable place.
2. You have now completed your new PhotoStory Project

Remember: For any other problems go to my site and I will sort them out A.S.A.P

www.pcprobsww.tk

www.ingramcontent.com/pod-product-compliance
Lightning Source LLC
Chambersburg PA
CBHW041148050326
40689CB00001B/533